W9-CUI-067

SPORTS' GREATEST OF ALL TIME

AUTO RACING'S
G.O.A.T.

DALE EARNHARDT, JIMMIE JOHNSON, AND MORE

JOE LEVIT

Lerner Publications ◆ Minneapolis

Lerner Publications Company
A division of Lerner Publishing Group, Inc.
241 First Avenue North
Minneapolis, MN 55401 USA

For reading levels and more information, look up this title at www.lernerbooks.com.

Main body text set in Aptifer Sans LT Pro.
Typeface provided by Linotype AG.

Library of Congress Cataloging-in-Publication Data

Names: Levit, Joseph, author.
Title: Auto racing's G.O.A.T. : Dale Earnhardt, Jimmie Johnson, and more / Joe Levit.
Other titles: Auto racing's greatest of all time
Description: Minneapolis : Lerner Publications, [2020] | Series: Sports' greatest of all time | Includes bibliographical references and index. | Audience: Age 7–11. | Audience: Grade 4 to 6.
Identifiers: LCCN 2018048868 (print) | LCCN 2018051910 (ebook) | ISBN 9781541556379 (eb pdf) | ISBN 9781541556034 (lb : alk. paper) | ISBN 9781541574403 (pb : alk. paper) | ISBN 9781541556379 (ebook PDF)
Subjects: LCSH: Automobile racing drivers—Biography—Juvenile literature. | Automobile racing drivers—Rating of—Juvenile literature. | Automobile racing—Juvenile literature. | Earnhardt, Dale, 1951–2001—Juvenile literature. | Johnson, Jimmie, 1975—Juvenile literature.
Classification: LCC GV1032.A1 (ebook) | LCC GV1032.A1 L47 2020 (print) | DDC 796.720922 [B]—dc23

LC record available at https://lccn.loc.gov/2018048868

Manufactured in the United States of America
1-46059-43475-3/5/2019

CONTENTS

Most NASCAR events feature more than forty drivers racing for the finish line.

START YOUR ENGINES!

FACTS AT A GLANCE

NIGEL MANSELL is the only driver to hold both the F1 (Formula 1) and IndyCar titles at one time.

MICHAEL SCHUMACHER ranks first in league history with seven F1 championships.

JIMMIE JOHNSON'S seven NASCAR championships are tied for the most of all time.

MARIO ANDRETTI is the only person to win the Driver of the Year award in three different decades.

Have you ever tried to make a list of the greatest auto racing drivers of all time? The world's best drivers race in F1, IndyCar, and NASCAR events. That's why the leagues are so popular with racing fans.

Drivers get points when they finish races. F1 rules award 25 points to the winner of each race and 18 points to the second-place driver, with fewer points awarded from there. The other leagues have similar systems. The driver with the most points at the end of the season wins the championship.

NASCAR, IndyCar, and F1 all feature superfast cars. But the leagues have many differences too. F1 and IndyCar use open-wheel vehicles. The wheels are outside of the cars' narrow bodies. Stock car wheels turn inside wide, bulky bodies.

Many F1 and IndyCar tracks have twists, turns, and sharp corners. Some races are on closed public roads. Most NASCAR races are on large oval tracks. Cars in all the leagues zoom for hours during races, often going 200 miles (321 km) per hour or faster.

Some pro drivers focus on F1 throughout their careers. Others prefer NASCAR or IndyCar. A select few have won in all three leagues. But just 10 drivers can be the G.O.A.T.—the greatest of all time.

IndyCar officially began in 1994, but the sport of open-wheel racing goes back more than 100 years.

F1 cars, shown here, look similar to Indy cars, but there are many differences in parts and rules that set the leagues apart.

You may disagree with the order of these rankings. Maybe you think some great drivers are missing. Amazing racers such as Lewis Hamilton, Scott Dixon, and Jim Clark failed to make it to the finish line. Your friends might have different rankings too. It's okay to disagree. Thinking about great race car drivers and forming your own opinions about them is what this book is all about.

#10

NIGEL MANSELL

Nigel Mansell raced F1 cars for 15 years. His aggressive driving style annoyed many opponents. He tried to gain an advantage by intimidating other racers. Mansell rarely took his foot off the gas pedal, and he wasn't afraid to take risks. That's why fans called him the British Bulldog.

Mansell's forceful style was successful, but it had a price. He won 31 F1 races during his 15-year career, and he crashed 32 times. One crash left him with a broken neck. Another broke a bone in his back.

Despite Mansell's injuries, he always raced with his all-out style. He won the 1992 F1 world championship. Looking for a new challenge, he soon left F1 to try IndyCar. In 1993, he won the IndyCar championship. That made him the only person to hold the F1 and IndyCar titles at the same time.

NIGEL MANSELL STATS

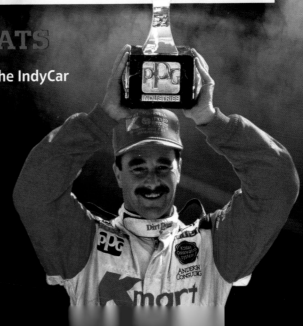

▶ He became the first driver to win the IndyCar championship in his first season.

▶ He ranks seventh all time with 31 wins in F1 races.

▶ He ranks 11th all time with 59 F1 podium appearances.

▶ He earned the pole position for 14 of 16 races in 1992.

▶ He joined the International Motorsports Hall of Fame in 2005

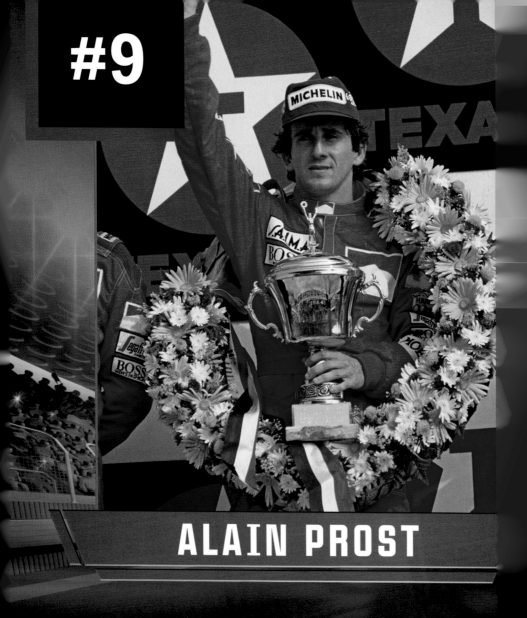

#9

ALAIN PROST

Alain Prost carefully planned his moves on the racetrack. Thinking ahead earned him the nickname the Professor. Prost would cruise below his top speed at the start of a race. He tried to prevent wearing down the car's brakes and tires. That way he could take fewer pit stops near the

Prost's approach to racing helped him outsmart and outrace the competition. He barely lost the 1984 F1 championship, finishing 0.5 points behind Niki Lauda. It marked the beginning of an incredible run of success. Prost won the F1 title in 1985, 1986, and 1989.

In 1992, Prost stepped away from the driver's seat. He spent the year as a racing analyst on TV. He returned to the track in 1993 and proved that the time away hadn't slowed him down. He won seven races and his fourth F1 championship that year.

ALAIN PROST STATS

▶ He won the F1 championship four times.

▶ He ranks fourth all time with 51 F1 race wins.

▶ He ranks fourth all time with 106 F1 podium appearances.

▶ He won the pole position for 13 of 16 races in 1993.

▶ Media members and sports legends honored him as the best auto racer of the 20th century in 1999.

#8

MICHAEL SCHUMACHER

Michael Schumacher was aggressive. Sometimes he bumped the car ahead of him, forcing other drivers to get out of his way or risk a crash. His incredible desire to succeed drove Schumacher on and off the track. He worked out in a gym every day to stay in shape. He prepared his body for long F1 races that might tire other drivers.

Schumacher is the most successful F1 driver of all time. In 2002, he became the only driver in history to reach the podium in every race of a season. He also broke the record for most podium appearances in a row with 19. He set the record for most wins in a season with 13 in 2004. Schumacher has won 22 different grand prix events, more than any other racer. And his 15 straight seasons with a grand prix win is the longest streak ever.

MICHAEL SCHUMACHER STATS

- His seven F1 championships are the most ever.

- He ranks first all time with 91 F1 wins.

- He ranks first all time with 155 F1 podium appearances.

- He won the pole position in 11 of 17 races in 2001.

- He won the World Sportsman of the Year

JIMMIE JOHNSON

Jimmie Johnson often positions himself just behind the leaders through the early laps of a race. He stays close, but he doesn't try to take the lead right away. At the very end of a race, Johnson makes his move. This strategy has helped make him incredibly successful. He is tied with Dale Earnhardt and Richard Petty for the most NASCAR championships of all time. Johnson is the only driver in history to win five NASCAR championships in a row.

In 2006, Johnson raced in NASCAR's biggest event, the Daytona 500. He took the lead with 14 laps remaining in the 200-lap race. One by one, drivers such as Ryan Newman tried to overtake Johnson. But he held them off to win the race. Johnson won the Daytona 500 again in 2013.

JIMMIE JOHNSON STATS

▶ He has won the NASCAR championship seven times.

▶ He has 83 NASCAR wins, tied for sixth most all-time wins.

▶ He has won the pole position for a NASCAR race 35 times.

▶ He won the Associated Press Male Athlete of the Year award in 2009.

▶ He has won the Driver of the Year award seven times.

#6

DALE EARNHARDT

Dale Earnhardt is one of the most popular auto racers of all time. His aggressive style made him a fan favorite. He was so determined to win that he sometimes scraped against other cars. His fierce driving forced his opponents to pay attention to him at all times. It also made many of them nervous. Fans and drivers called him the Intimidator.

Earnhardt raced in his first Daytona 500 in 1979. He finally won the celebrated race in 1998. Three years later, he died in a crash at Daytona. Traveling faster than 150 miles (241 km) per hour during the final lap, Earnhardt lost control of his car and hit a wall. Moments later, his son, Dale Earnhardt Jr., finished the race in second place. Earnhardt was one of the first people inducted into the NASCAR Hall of Fame when it opened in 2010.

DALE EARNHARDT STATS

▶ He won the NASCAR championship seven times.

▶ He had **76 NASCAR wins**, the eighth most of all time.

▶ He earned the pole position for a NASCAR race **22 times**.

▶ He finished a NASCAR race **281 times** in the top five.

▶ He finished a NASCAR race **428 times** in the top 10.

AYRTON SENNA

Ayrton Senna was a brilliant and daring F1 racer. Though his car had many gears, Senna had just one—full speed ahead. F1 keeps track of the leader of every lap in a race. Senna was in first place for an amazing 36 percent of the laps he drove in his career. In 1988, Senna won his first F1 world championship. He went on to win two more championships in the next three years.

Senna drove fast under any conditions. He was just as comfortable racing his car in the rain as he was on a dry track. That helped him win wet F1 races such as the 1985 Grand Prix of Portugal and the 1993 European Grand Prix. He won at least 12 important races in the rain. Senna's life ended at the age of 34 in a crash at the 1994 San Marino Grand Prix.

AYRTON SENNA STATS

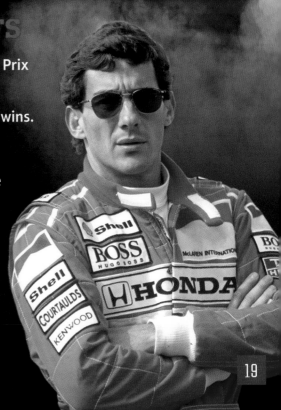

- He holds the record for Monaco Grand Prix victories with six wins.

- He ranks fifth all time with 41 F1 race wins.

- He had 80 F1 podium appearances.

- He ranks third all time with 65 F1 pole positions.

- He won eight of the 16 F1 events in 1988.

RICHARD PETTY

Richard Petty raced for 35 years and became NASCAR's most successful driver. That's why racing fans and fellow drivers call him the King. Petty holds the record for most victories in a season by winning 27 races in 1967. That year he set the record for wins in a row with 10.

Petty competed in 1,184 NASCAR races. He won 200 of them, an all-time record. That's almost double the total wins of David Pearson, the next closest racer. Petty set another record by finishing second in a race 157 times. He also won the Daytona 500 a record seven times.

Petty raced for decades despite having a few major crashes. In 1970, he crashed at the Rebel 400 in Darlington, South Carolina, and injured his shoulder. Then safety netting was added on all stock car windows to prevent such injuries.

RICHARD PETTY STATS

▶ He won the NASCAR championship seven times.

▶ His 1,184 races are the most in NASCAR history.

▶ He earned the pole position for a NASCAR race 123 times.

▶ He was in the lead for 51,406 laps in his career, an all-time record.

▶ He joined the NASCAR Hall of Fame in 2010.

JUAN MANUEL FANGIO

As a young driver, Juan Manuel Fangio raced in long-distance events in South America. The races covered thousands of miles and could last for weeks. The long distances helped him build strength and stamina. Fangio didn't begin racing in F1 until he was 39 years old.

He used his racing experience to master a move called the four-wheel drift. The driver slides the car sideways around a turn in the road, helping the car go faster around the curve.

Fangio's F1 career was brief but incredibly successful. In his seven full F1 seasons, he was the champion five times. He finished second in his other two seasons.

Fangio was leading the 1957 German Grand Prix late in the race. But he lost the lead after a slow pit stop. He drove the fastest lap in the track's history to come back and win the race. Some F1 fans call it the greatest racing performance of all time.

JUAN MANUEL FANGIO STATS

- ▶ He won six of the eight races he entered in 1954.

- ▶ He won 24 of the 51 F1 races he entered in his career, the best winning percentage in F1 history.

- ▶ He had 35 F1 podium appearances.

- ▶ He earned the pole position in 29 of his 51 races, the best percentage in history.

- ▶ In 1957, he became the oldest driver to win the F1 championship at 46 years and 41 days old.

A. J. FOYT

One way for a driver to become great is to win different types of races. A. J. Foyt showed he could win fast-paced races such as the 500-mile (804 km) Daytona 500. He also could drive thousands of miles and win an endurance race such as 24 Hours of Le Mans.

Foyt is the only driver to win the Indianapolis 500, the Daytona 500, 24 Hours of Daytona, and 24 Hours of Le Mans. Besides open-wheel racing and stock cars, Foyt raced smaller vehicles such as sprint cars. Foyt's 67 wins are the most in IndyCar history. From 1958 to 1992, he set a record by racing in 35 straight Indy 500s. He won the race four times. He also won seven NASCAR events in his career, including the 1972 Daytona 500.

A. J. FOYT STATS

▶ He finished an IndyCar race in the top five 144 times.

▶ In 1964, he won 10 of the season's 13 IndyCar races.

▶ His seven IndyCar championships are the most ever.

▶ He earned the pole position 53 times during his IndyCar career.

▶ The Associated Press voted him Driver of the Century in 1999 in a tie with Mario Andretti.

MARIO ANDRETTI

Mario Andretti grew up admiring great F1 racers such as Alberto Ascari. Yet Andretti raced in many different leagues before becoming an F1 driver himself. He started his career in vehicles such as sprint cars that don't go as

When Andretti started competing with faster cars, he proved to be the greatest auto racer of all time. In a career that lasted nearly 30 years, Andretti dominated the competition on the sport's biggest stages. He won the Daytona 500 in 1967 and the Indianapolis 500 in 1969. He started racing in F1 events in 1968. He became the F1 world champion 10 years later. He is the only driver to win the Indianapolis 500, the Daytona 500, and the F1 title.

MARIO ANDRETTI STATS

▶ He won 12 Hours of Sebring, a yearly endurance race, three times.

▶ He won the Driver of the Year award in 1967, 1978, and 1984.

▶ He is one of three drivers to win a race on a public road, a paved track, and a dirt track in one season.

▶ He won the IndyCar championship four times.

▶ The Associated Press voted him Driver of the Century in 1999 in a tie with A. J. Foyt.

YOUR
G.O.A.T.

IT'S YOUR TURN TO MAKE A G.O.A.T. LIST ABOUT PRO RACE CAR DRIVERS. Get in the race by starting with some research. Carefully consider the rankings in this book. Then check out the Further Information section on page 31. You'll see books and websites that will tell you more about the top drivers of the past and present. Search online for more about auto racing. Or talk to a librarian about other resources. You could even try reaching out to some of racing's top drivers to see what they think.

Think it over and make your top 10 list of the greatest racers of all time. Do you have friends who like auto racing? Ask them to make their own lists and compare them. Which drivers do you have that no one else listed? Are you missing a driver that your friends think everyone should include? Talk it over, and try to convince them that your list is the G.O.A.T.!

AUTO RACING FACTS

▶ Indianapolis Motor Speedway in Indiana, home of the Indianapolis 500, is nicknamed the Brickyard because the track used to be made of bricks.

▶ When it reaches 200 miles (321 km) per hour, a race car travels almost the length of a football field in one second.

▶ In his long career, racer Terry Labonte set an all-time record by driving more than 14,892 miles (23,966 km) during the Daytona 500. That equals 5,957 laps!

▶ Top F1 pit crews can refuel a car and change its tires in three seconds.

▶ F1 tracks are full of turns, so drivers use their brakes a lot. During a race, the brake discs get hot. They can reach the same average temperature as molten lava!

GLOSSARY

Daytona 500: a yearly 500-mile (804 km) race that is NASCAR's most famous event

endurance race: an auto race that tests a driver's ability to race for a long time

grand prix: a single race that is part of an international series of races

Indianapolis 500: a yearly 500-mile race that is IndyCar's most famous event

pit stop: a stop during a race to refuel and change a car's tires

podium appearance: when a driver finishes in the top three in a race

pole position: the car in the best position at the beginning of a race. The pole position is usually awarded to the fastest driver during qualifying laps before the race.

sprint car: a midsize race car that usually drives on a dirt track

24 Hours of Daytona: a yearly endurance race in Daytona Beach, Florida, that lasts 24 hours

winning percentage: races won divided by the total number of races entered

FURTHER INFORMATION

Jimmie Johnson
https://www.jimmiejohnson.com/

Kiddle—Auto Racing Facts for Kids
https://kids.kiddle.co/Auto_racing

Monnig, Alex. *Behind the Wheel of an Indy Car.* Mankato, MN: Child's World, 2016.

Nagelhout, Ryan. *Talk like a Race Car Driver.* New York: Gareth Stevens, 2017.

Savage, Jeff. *Auto Racing Super Stats.* Minneapolis: Lerner Publications, 2018.

Sports Illustrated Kids—More Sports
https://www.sikids.com/more-sports

INDEX

PHOTO ACKNOWLEDGMENTS

Image credits: Action Sports Photography/Shutterstock.com, p. 4; HodagMedia/ Shutterstock.com, p. 6; Ev. Safronov/Shutterstock.com, p. 7; Allsport/Getty Images, p. 8; RacingOne/Getty Images, p. 9 (right); Bob Thomas/Getty Images, p. 10; Paul-Henri Cahier/Getty Images, pp. 9 (left), 11 (left); JARNOUX Patrick/Paris Match/Getty Images, p. 11 (right); Steve Etherington/EMPICS/Getty Images, p. 12; Marcus Brandt/Bongarts/Getty Images, p. 13 (left); Pascal Rondeau/Getty Images, p. 13 (right); Jared C. Tilton/Stringer/Getty Images, p. 14; Nick Laham/Stringer/ Getty Images, pp. 15 (both); BRIAN CLEARY/Stringer/Getty Images, p. 16; Robert Alexander/Getty Images, p. 17 (left); Joe Robbins/Getty Images, p. 17 (right); Pascal Rondeau/Allsport/Getty Images, p. 18; Jean-Marc LOUBAT/Gamma-Rapho/ Getty Images, p. 19 (left); Mike Hewitt/Allsport/Getty Images, p. 19 (right); Focus on Sport/Getty Images, pp. 20, 21 (both); Bernard Cahier/Getty Images, p. 22; Angelo Cozzi/Mondadori Portfolio/Getty Images, p. 23 (right); ullstein bild Dtl./ Shell/Getty Images, p. 23 (right); Bob Harmeyer/Archive Photos/Getty Images, pp. 24, 26, 27 (both); David Madison/Getty Images, p. 25 (right); Owen C. Shaw/ Getty Images, p. 25 (right); liewluck/Shutterstock.com, p. 28. Design elements: EFKS/Shutterstock.com (arena); conrado/Shutterstock.com (smoke); lscatel/ Shutterstock.com (starburst).

Cover: Robert Alexander/Archive Photos/Getty Images (Dale Earnhardt Sr.); Brian Lawdermilk/Getty Images (Jimmie Johnson).